THE FLESH ENVELOPE

The Flesh Envelope

poems by
Susan Luzzaro

West End Press

Some of these poems have previously appeared in the following publications: *American Poetry Review, americas review, Centennial Review, Critique of America/Arete, Hayden's Ferry Review, Iowa Review, Kalliope, Malahat Review, Negative Capability, Puerto Del Sol, Quarterly West, 13th Moon, Wisconsin Review.*

The author wishes to thank the Los Angeles Arts Council for the generous art scholarship which enabled her to complete her Master of Fine Arts degree.

First edition, March 1998
ISBN 0-931122-88-0

Front cover montage by Myrna Dearie
Back cover photograph by Frank Luzzaro
Cover design and book design by Michael Reed
Typography by Prototype, Albuquerque, NM

Distributed by the University of New Mexico Press

West End Press • P.O. Box 27334 • Albuquerque, New Mexico 87125

In loving memory for
Melvin & Katherine Heine

Contents

1

1

And this poetry will have to be acrid with knowledge and bitter with longing to have the power to trouble people's sleep. For we are sleeping, we are sleepers, out of fear of having to look at ourselves and our world.

—Ingeborg Bachmann

Who has twisted us around like this, so that no matter what we do, we are in the posture of someone going away?

—Rainer Maria Rilke

Abandon & Possession

In the time of the butterfly,
in the time of the black-winged, henna-dipped Lorquin's Admiral,
the field is swept by yellow,
yellow blossoms of tobacco tree,
yellow petals of deer vetch,
yellow puffballs of charlock,
& the yellow of sweet fennel—
in the distance a city truck is shredding
thousands of lemon eucalyptus leaves,
even the air consents to be yellow—

in the manner of spring trees are planting themselves in the field—

& if you are a child of five this tangle of green stems, of woody stems,
these yellow faces taller than you, bearing a single brown eye down on you—
are the stuff of beauty, the stuff of terror—
& if you are a girl of fourteen or twenty
the field is the face of your lover, is
abandon & possession, is the bouquet of your heart—
but if you are a woman of forty
the field is the field
& it is not calling itself yellow
& it is not articulating the word flower—
rather, it is dreaming its own dream
in which it allows a woman, neither fecund nor sterile, to walk.

The Flesh Envelope

The soul is a body of fine particles distributed throughout the frame.

—Epicurus

Folded into this fleshy envelope,
this frame that eats too much, drinks too much,
loves immoderately, angers easily & seldom forgives,
this husk that drives stupidly & works erratically—

is a Garden & in that Garden a soul
that walks at a leisured pace
discussing moral existence with like-minded friends.
The Garden is bounded by slow-growing things
& the sweet fountain sound of reasoned discourse.
The mind is quiet there, extends itself
toward pure thought—the senses, too,
are groomed like fingernails—are clean, shiny, & useful.
In a place like this the soul has time
to brake for beauty, break the simplest of bread
& drink watered wine with an occasional pot of cheese—
exist like the gods of *intermundia*—
perfect & perfectly indifferent.
The soul is spending its life in such a way
that in the manner of Epicurus on his last day
it can climb into a bronze tub,
ask for an unwatered glass of wine,
& bid this world a serene goodbye.

The soul chafes in this horsehair body
which runs breakneck through each day—
this body that cannot dally long enough
to feel the kiss, taste the mushroom,
reason to the point of moral action.
It would if it could take its rhythm from the moon,
or lean long & heliotropic into the sun.
The body is hungry for a single carnal truth.
It is not dumb to Time's winged chariot,
it feels the whip, the lash, the bad knee, bad conscience,
but cheats the lesson. It sings
with Edith Piaf, "Je ne regrette rien,"
but regrets as many days as not—is sick at the speed of light.

Even an angel would refuse flesh.
How can I bring my soul into the world
without bringing the Garden?
The Garden is the apple, the world is the worm.
Or the soul is wax, the body pure flame.

Begin with the Body

i cry until they let me take my underpants off step towards it it is all moving
it is in & out cold covers my feet put my hand in laugh it looks like fish
open my legs water rushes into folds & cubbies leaves crunchies in my holes

it was hot it was june they said anyway i could not run without a shirt
i cried i had no breasts they said ok run with shirt unbuttoned but next year
button up i felt wind & sun especial on my chest next summer felt men's eyes

lay in the bottom bunk when you are home sick she said she thought it was
stomach flu i held myself down there moved my fingers gentle in the folds
on the spot panicked when i found blood she said god was punishing me

then he said he could tell if ever i was with someone else my vagina would
be different then he told me what he would do if i ever then he put his hand
under my blouse my breasts begged i was afraid i would never get enough

when my father walked me down the hall that last morning i was dressed
in bell shaped lace off-white he knew still he told me i didn't have to go
to the church where people were already sitting what if he had told me sooner

nursing the babies was sexual little mouths sucking right breast left breast
uterus contracting tiny hands patting flesh bare bodies connected by more
than eye can see you have to be careful not to squeeze them back inside

ate for all starving children became the mania of a cleaned plate grew big
as a house children could break whole pieces from me & did rode the danger
of no horse no wave no lover i was bonemaking marrow i was milk i was mother

watching daughter ten coup de pieds hand gripping bar lithe silhouette
i was still young you couldn't tell by me began to walk to dance but never in a
pirouette did i like the body turned to me some men said they did so i let them

surprise i find i can still run fast ignite self create heat enter winter water
my heart i thought a flaccid sea anemone fingered once too often comes alive
an audience a bell clapping

Hummingbird in Winter

This poem is for the unrecycled '50s—
for white bread smeared with margarine & layered with white sugar—
a chief source of sustenance when I was young—
this poem is for October 1957 & my father, perhaps prouder, perhaps happier
than he will ever be, driving home in his Ford station wagon a Miller High Life
between his thighs & a new TV in the back of the car—
& for my friends & me who ever after instead of playing hide & seek, or freeze-tag,
or statue-maker, would watch Johnny Downs dance on a milk bottle,
or Annette Funicello, with her incongruous full breasts & Mickey Mouse ears
become the teenager we would all die to become.
This poem is for my mother who died believing Velveeta was cheese
& never discovered garlic.
This poem has trees to burn, is secular, synthetic sass.
This poem is for nights & days I have lain on my back, my mind
jammed in a single washing cycle—rinse, rinse, rinse.
This poem is for the yellow-mouthed, bright red hummingbird feeders,
for the colored sugar water that enticed the hummingbird, frozen
on the second story ledge, to stay long into winter, way past instinct.
This poem is a tribute to the cool indifference of Styrofoam, plastic, atom,
the dream of perfectability.
This poem is the antithesis of nature, which like the rich man or the camel
will not pass through the eye of the needle.
This poem is for the heaven, white & treeless,
to which we are all driving in our automobiles.

Hands on the Wheel

Riding around in the truck
with Walt, the plumber,
I could see how life was simpler.
I might have gone down to the hardware store
& flirted, bribed or whined
when they told me they couldn't deliver
the cast iron tub for a week.
Walt said we'd just go get it,
use leverage to load it up.
When he lit another Pall Mall
from the pack rolled in his sleeve,
I began to happily tap the empties
on the floor & forget about cancer & death & all.
To ride up front was to ride with my uncles,
to enter that masculine domain—they could
flush a deer out of the scrub brush
on any hill & we would ride home
in the dusk with a doe or buck across the hood,
& though I did not like the deer so limp & wasted,
wasted as my father is now,
still I liked being in the presence
of power & know-how—in my father's presence
no truck, no bike, no engine, no tire
was irretrievable, as he is now,
he could fix every & anything,
not in a professional way, you understand,
but in a makeshift way like Walt—

so I admired the dust on the radio knobs
agreed as to how old lyrics could lodge
between you & a good night's sleep—
we were both thinking very elemental
smelling the ancient cat piss wafting up
from the back of the truck,
Walt had so many cats he lost count—
when he turned to me & said
Hey, little lady, see that phone on the dashboard,
you could call Tokyo from here.
& I smiled in spite of everything
to be beside a man with his hands on the wheel
of the whole fixable world.

Silver Bow

I am the great chief who makes people ashamed.
                    —Kwakiutl song

My mother's fragile hand holds
the ornament to the light.
The doorbell rings & God's omniscient voice
should tell her "Don't answer; go on,
hang the crystal bell on the Christmas tree."
But she will answer—& lose
her beauty & her pride
to the Lutheran Women's Auxiliary—
who pile canned cranberries, a frozen turkey
& gaily wrapped gifts beneath the tree.
Among the presents, a donated doll's house
before which I have lain many times
with a friend & I moved the perfect little figurines
through all the many rooms.
I want my mother to refuse,
but she never will, her house
will grow small about her
& when she returns to church
on Sunday she will not be so proud
of her six children.

Instead the underbelly
of every gift, the eyes of every giver,
every occasion for gift giving
has become like some lavish tribal Potlach
where like the Kwakiutl
we are vanquished by a gift.

The Distance

Through the whole of our small town
my brother could be seen—
hair tan as thistle,
shoe heels all walked over,
following his homing pigeons home.
The boy who never learned to read
or ride a two-wheeler
or write the name "Dan"
found his domain in a walk-in cage
beneath the orange honeysuckle tree.
While my brothers & sisters & I
pinched bees in those bright blossoms
& wheeled off on bikes to "sting" our enemies,
Dan memorized the habits of his greys,
the history of his tumblers,
& the day & the distance from which
every pigeon returned to him.
The feathered ritual of courtships,
the pecking order of the wooden dowel
became his custom & convention.
He dreamed their marriages,
organized each exodus & return,
baptized their progeny
in a shallow silver trough.
Like any too exclusive love
he became obsessive, angry
if they mated out of a preference
other than his own. First,
he only broke their eggs,
then he wrung their necks.
Sentenced for life to a halfway house
most days are broken up by
cigarettes, sodas & meds—
an occasional visit, or a little gift
nothing Dan could ever follow home—
gerbil, goldfish, turtle—
wingless & dreamless.

Black Slip

With the innocence of routine
I passed through the chain-link fence
& entered the sandbox. Whatever
a child my age could know was altered,
prefigured, by an image—Penny Linton,
a fourth grader who lived
in the trailer park behind the school,
doubled over in the cold sand
wearing nothing but a woman's black slip.

Say it was her mother's—
slipped over her head by her mother's lover—
say that Penny was hungry for touch—
& her mother returned early
from bartending & called
only her daughter sick & beat her
with an electrical cord
& threw her out of the trailer.
How could I know this—
unless it happened to me,
or something like this happened
to someone like me.

I did what I could that morning—
never let my eyes meet Penny's—
never let her know
that what you see can change you—so—
that I would put on
the sheen & lace of a black silk slip—
that it would open me
to every conceivable abandonment.

Or let me tell it another way—
that I was only a witness—
that young as I was I sensed
there was something in this cataclysm for Penny—
a purging of her own powers of desire—
a reenactment she must perform
again & again—of the loss of love.

That later in life
I would succumb to & resist
the electricity of touch,
the eroticism of whisper,
warm breath lifting every tiny hair—
the seductive love of sequential lovers—

or conversely keep all desire
in a box—the size of a conjugal bedroom—
where a black slip might be
                    the sad flag of defeat.

Pagan Rites

I taste wild strawberries
& I am 14 & creeping
from my parents' tent,
their watchful eyes hooded with sleep.
With Dwayne & Chuck & Sarah
I scour the hills   ankles scraped by weeds
hands touching   soft rich earth
strong slow bark   each other—
all things as if they were,
all things because they are,
first & last.
& death is a fine net wisp
a veil on the moon, existing only
to heighten our moments.
By a fire we dance pagan steps,
uncoded from the prints on our feet,
as the sun rises we pillage & loot,
breakfasting on strawberries, nuts & beer.

　　Now my own children turn wild
dilated eyes on me, waiting
for a lapse in attention, waiting
for a taste of wild strawberries.
I will my eyes to close, my grip to slacken,
as I see them slip out
with a band of young friends,
to a time before fields, plows, or the care
of domestic crops, to a place that is not
Eden—but Earth.

Fin de Siecle

My son is suicidal.
Death roots in his
beautiful body
like datura
in dry ground.
Raised by me
to imagine what might be,
he cannot accept what is.
It is unacceptable.
He writes on the walls
of his room. He records
the death of his cat,
the death of his grandfather,
the deaths from apartheid.
He has posted on one wall
his draft registration;
beneath it, like inches of growth,
he has marked the progress of "Star Wars."
His walls are a metaphor
for his mind, his mind
a metaphor for this world.
He lies on his bed
as if on a bier.
He is pure, vegetarian,
weightless & ascending.
His thin, slate face,
heaven-pointed,
slices me to the bone.
I have no image
to counter the skulls
that flower like nightshade
from the T-shirts
of his friends.
I have no insignia
to antedate the spikes
that rise like angry thorns
from the sleeves

of their black jackets.
If once I dreamed of
saving the world,
in this dead decade
I will count myself lucky
to save my own son.

Side to Side

In the seventeenth summer of her life
my daughter is learning to drive.
Morning sun burns through the windshield
& the wide sash of the belt
cuts between our breasts.
A dark tongue of sweat
sticks us to our seat
as we circle round & round
the old neighborhood.
We practice starting, stopping,
beneath the aging pepper tree,
we practice backing up between two palms.
Slowly I unclutch the dashboard,
gradually my foot stops pressing
imaginary brakes. The delicate
balance of power shifts
from side to side—suddenly
my life is in her hands—
& now each lap around I see
my daughter growing taller,
blonder & more confident—as if
this windshield were some hourglass
& all my sand had shifted.

Toxic Face

You have an obscene number
of moisturizers, my daughter announces.
It's true. I have day creams & night creams,
ions & microspheres, pore perfecters, creams
to nourish the skin, creams
to protect from the evil ways of UVAs, UVBs—
I have peel-offs, 10-minute masques, firmers, uplifters—
I have indulged in the organic, the high-tech,
one even claims placenta as an ingredient.
At this moment I have the latest,
the hottest on my face—hyaluronic acid—
imagine visible improvement in two weeks.

My daughter & I find me incongruous—
the same woman who encouraged her
to grow hair on her legs, hair under her arms,
the same woman empowered by wispy brown curls
escaping the underarm of her sleeveless blouse—
that is to say *me,* a middle-aged woman,
has turned her face into a hothouse,
hydro-technic, hydroponic experiment
in the irreversible reversibility—of age.
Vanessa, my daughter, suggests delicately—
You cannot erase wrinkles short of surgery.

Still I lay my depression dollars down
at the carnival of any mall—
you can sell me turtle oil, shark oil, snake oil—
(till recently when I began to correctly eschew
products with hydrolisized animal parts).
Because to succumb to something small as a wrinkle,
an incidental fissure, a cicatrix of time—
is to buy into the linear idea—
my skin is a one-way ticket,
my skin is on a runaway train,
my skin is a gold lamé bag
carrying my heart, my lungs,
my breasts, my sex, my every valuable

away. Away from the inchoate ecstasy
of the epidermis, away from
the absolute pleasure of fingertips on flesh,
from everything & everyone I fiercely hate or love—
from Vanessa, true bloom of my life,
who tells me *skin is the largest organ of the body*
as she smothers me in her young flesh.

Partial & Peculiar

Tonight my children choose
the story *Once Upon A River.*
At the end of the book
we spread a fold-out nature page
across our knees. There,
where the fallen oak bridges
the stream, our fingers trace
the circle where the proud
kingfisher once sat. Five circles,
five black mourning bands, mark
the vanished or endangered species.

Likewise, I tell the story
of a red-haired man who once
lifted their chubby, froggy bodies
over his head & called them
my prince, my princess.
Years from now I will finish
the story when I tell them
how this man, cornered by the FBI,
chose his own death over Vietnam or jail.
My words work to etch images
indelible as skeletons
pressed into stratified rock.

No litany of absences,
I tell the story, too,
of the partial & peculiar ways
these losses reverse themselves.
From the dry hill behind our house,
the once endangered mountain lion
creeps down to munch small poodles.
& at La Jolla Cove the ungainly brown pelicans
repossess Bird Rock.
But for myself I keep
the uncanny joy I feel,
when across the crowded room I see
the smile of a dead friend
on a stranger's face.

2

The profound seriousness and urgency of human thought about justice arises from the awareness that we all really need the things that justice distributes, and need them for life itself.

—Martha Nussbaum

Writing is kin to utopia. That is, it has a painful yet joyous yen for the absolute.
—Christa Woolf

Meditation On Politics & Death

If you walked out of the city
imagining a better world,
a world where choice & knowledge
played some larger part,
& you carried with you
a *Field Guide to Edible Plants and Mushrooms*
while your god or atheism slid
into a dream of meaning,
then, perhaps, when arrested
in a field by some uncertain growth,
you, too, would think of
the undocumented workers
who not far from here
& out of a hunger foreign to you or me
fried up the wrong kind of mushrooms—
died writhing in pain.
Like you I am a stranger
to hunger but not to the chaos of death,
to sudden, irrevocable, unjust loss.
Together we might lose faith in
our annotated colored plates
when we saw how the earth
moist as coffee grounds
parted to let a whiteness rise
which was wholly indifferent
to our need, or lack of it—
we might marvel how
the indifference of nature
is so like the indifference
of man to man. We might
for the thousandth time
wonder at the point of
choice without knowledge,
life without everlasting.
Disenchanted, the book
would slide from our hand as we reached
toward the sumac—uncertain
whether the red berry
was the poison or the cure.

El Otro Lado

Midnight,
no wind,
still the acacia shivers.
Mother knows who the leaves
conceal, she knows
who banged the door.
She heard them whispering
beneath her bedroom window
in some quick foreign tongue—
she knows what they want
& she knows that they steal,
they steal.

The hot night gathers & rolls
in drops down my father's neck.
He peers through wrought iron bars,
sees shadows in flux.
A small wind lifts the tendrils
from his neck—it feels like fear.
He knows what they want
& he knows that they steal,
they steal.

& how can I sleep
while the helicopter hovers
flushing the field
with its circle of light?
& how can I sleep
when beneath the dense cover
of the pepper tree
a man lies dreaming
my father's nightmare?
Beneath the dark bridge of the night
in trucks & trunks, for a fee, for blood,
through arroyos & sewers,
through a cut in the fence,
carrying green net bags
& letters in their shoes

to an uncle in Fresno—
Alejandro, Luisa, Alfonso
are coming—
quiet as blood they are flowing
out of the dark gash
between countries.
Stealing, stealing back home.

Milagro

This is how I am. How many of my friends are.
Two minds, a welter of impulses—intelligent,
but inclined toward signs, feathers, divinations.
Newspapers arrive with too much, too little news—
the human tragedy, the five food groups, the globe
glutted with power & grief. I try to translate
twenty-six letters into a cosmology
in which I can believe, but three sets of insistent
yellow eyes peer in at me.

                           At first I think
they are messengers, divine, electric blue & black,
cawing from the pepper tree, twice the size of scrub jays.
How could anything be blown so far off course,
come from below the Sonora to this clapboard house
& not carry a message?

                         I ponder the symbols.
Why three? (They should be in pairs.) Why this exotic
arrival in midwinter? I barter peanuts
for revelations, cheese & raisins for uncommon
wisdom. The cock of the head, the arc of the flight
might be prophetic, might foreshadow.

                        But like gods
the Beechy's Jays become too demanding, peck at my
bedroom window at 6 a.m. instead of 7,
squawk "Come here, Sue, feed me." This is a command
I have responded to all my life. Feeding is
my medium—the peanut my surest message—till
one day their beautiful plumes feather the ground—
they seem listless, possibly ill. A woman from
the Audubon tells me she thinks the birds are
illegal—did not fly here, but crossed the border
hidden in a cake pan, garbage bag, or false panel.

This is the way of it, I think, the way some
miracles arrive—their plumage too bright for
belief—their speech too difficult for translation,
their origins disputed. Perched on the jacaranda,
they tap out messages in a celestial code.
The answers cannot be lived out on this earth.

Fräulein Heine

At the party there was
bratwurst & cabbage,
huge steins of beer
& an accordion player
who made music for hours.
Most of the night
I was pinned to the wall
by an older man, his blue eyes
blazing in an aging face.
Because my maiden name
was Heine & his first name
was Fritz, I waited
for a kind of recognition to rise
in the keepsake of my blood.
I listened for words like *schlafen*
or *vergessen* that had gentled
my own father's speech.
Then we danced a polka
& I thought I liked
the man's firm hand
on my back, the decisive
one, two, three of his feet,
telling me just so
& never otherwise.
Until my desire to please
disfigured me in my own eyes,
& he leaned closer to whisper
yet another good, old story—
how at seventeen he joined
the National Socialists.
My feet thickened,
my tongue became dry ice.
All my life I have needed to know
that I would hide a stranger,
carry leaflets, sabotage a munitions plant—
not let fear nor love
turn me from my purpose.
Yet here I was, pliant as a girl
who did not know where guilt began—
dancing in the arms of a Nazi.

Nicola Sacco and Bartolomeo Vanzetti were political prisoners, falsely accused of murder and held by the state of Massachusetts for six years until they were executed in 1927.

Comrade

All night skunks rooted
our abandoned garden, Nico,
where once you brought
the most exotic buds to flower.
In sleep Dante & Ines groaned.
I groaned too, not for the smell
the skunks had unleashed, but
for the weight of those two lives,
their hands small as the birdwings
you tell me block your tiny patch of sky.
Today you called me *comrade*
& spoke to me of *anarchy & freedom,*
as if they were the children
we brought into this world.
It's hard, Nico, to embrace beliefs
where once your body lay.
In your absence I have even
thought of my old god & the wooden pews
I first pressed my body to.
I amaze myself to number
the principles I might renounce
just to have a neighbor speak to me.
But when they lead your tall body
down that last corridor, body
I had thought to lean on all my life,
when they slit your pants & cuff
your ankles to that chair, Nico,
when they cap your shaven head
with cold metal, husband
no more, I will call you comrade—
curse this capitalist country.

La Fleur Sauvage

We love variety.
We want every color,
every texture, every taste.
We want tulips from Holland
& cars from Germany.
We want summer fruits in winter
& winter vegetables in summer.
We want to vacation
on some farthest shore,
not to hear the sound
of our own language.
But come six o'clock
doors slam & curtains
slide on runners
like zippers over private parts.
We eat dinner in a closed circle.
We lie down in the same bed
with the same person of the same sex
& only the night is different.
Moisture drips
down our hothouse windows,
while outside
tendrils lasso the trellis
climbing rung by rung
to our bedrooms
& wildflowers ravage our dreams.

The Other

A painful bruise purples
like cabbage on my ass.
While I was jogging
a man in a red Toyota truck
reached out & slapped me.
What did he see
running beneath the eucalyptus—
a deer, a dog, only an ass?
Had he the time
he might have raped me,
if I had had a rock
I would have hurled it.

Once a man I loved raised himself
on one elbow to count my ribs
& say in jest: *Men want sex,
women want love.* What truth
I found in that old adage
I found lying beneath him.
As one of the women he saw
from time to time I felt his hand move
over my breasts, my thighs,
like rain over water.
I learned from him
not mystery—but anonymity.

& what is my part in this,
pressing these griefs to me
like thorns, pressing them
into the absolute ledger of my heart.
I lie down with men but never trust them.
I tell you this division is deeper than my own history—
deeper, at times, than my desire to mend.

Even before the speeding truck
was over the next hill, a handprint,
primitive as one on a cave wall,
began to surface on my skin.
Out of that same dark mentality,
out of prehistoric time,
my own arcane curse arose:

Every woman you lie with will be alien,
strange-colored, smell of damp places, mushrooms & caves.
Every woman will speak a tenderness
you will never hear. Afraid of the dark
you will always ejaculate prematurely.
You will lie down to sleep with,
you will die in, the arms of your enemy.

"On Every Vulva is Written the Name of the Man Destined to Enter"
(extracted from *Eye of the Sun*)

Like a Pennsylvania Dutch sign Wilcomen Hans,
or a big red flower with a minute black signature,
or invisible ink, moisture as a kind of litmus test—
in the intricacy of tiny veins a name might be scribbled.

How many names can dance on the lips of a vulva?
Must a woman's name be written in the obscurity of tea leaves?

So much is unanswered in aphorisms—
like the one about the birds in the bush—
what kind of birds are they anyway, are they wanted for food,
or for beauty, will the birds have to die?
Is the moral then something to do with possession?

Of course the one about the vulva is a lie—
disseminated in the wild hope
that women would believe it,
that they would be true to what had entered them—
be it animal, vegetable or mineral.
To enter sounds like a tunnel, there are
two sides to a tunnel, a person only passes through a tunnel,
a tunnel is a human construct, not a human.

I would love to believe that the metaphysical
is deeply implicated in the carnal—
the act of love as an act of faith—the one true tool
we were given to sort the wheat from the chaff—
yet destiny, we discover, is no more linked
to true love than it is to good sex.

Imagine the vulva as a kind of wedding ring,
elliptical instead of round, but bear with me—
if we wrap these sweet lips around you, do we get to keep you?
A name can't hold a person against his or her will—
marriage is a happy demonstration of that—or is it?
But there will be one in every crowd
who will want to leave an indelible mark,
the flame of a brand, the aesthetic of a tattoo—
can a name be expunged? Will it hurt?

Maybe just initials will do—
enclosed in a heart, pierced by an arrow—
lord, some kind of sign by which women can
distinguish the one who would make love
from the one who would make casual graffiti.

Sunday Evening

Fried squid on the plate, chianti in the glass
& on the stove water bubbling to a boil.
With Caruso I begin to sing "La Donna E Mobile,"
while garlic & pine nuts dance in olive oil.
Now jingling in my ear I hear the timpani
of silver earrings & feel the silken
swish of hem about my ankles, as I
glide deeper & deeper into abandon.
I dance, I sing out loud, clap my hands
& send patchouli rushing up my nose.
I eat with my fingrs, read at the table,
& caress the cat with my bare toes.
Later tonight when the candles sink
into themselves & I call it all success—
note this—I was high & I was having fun
& no man came to fill no emptiness.

Night Bloom

1.

In California there are poppies
that bloom only in the wake of a fire.
Elbowing aside the ashes,
they raise on thin green wicks
scarlet tokens of the flame.

2.

After the plutonium burst in Nagasaki,
after the temperature exceeded $6{,}000°$ C,
the vegetation ran wild.
A tree dormant for twelve years
burst into fiery buds in late August.
Morning glories, driven mad
by radiation, split sidewalks,
covered walls & bloomed
from the mouths of drainpipes & teapots.
Poppies emerged with full cups of blood.

3.

As children we learn to believe
in what we have yet to see.
In 1957, when I was nine,
I built a bomb shelter in my backyard.
With my father's tools
I hollowed out the old garden.
I covered my pit with an abandoned trellis,
an old tarp & clods of loose soil.
On the first spring night
I slept out. Beneath a layer of dirt
& two green army blankets
I was cut off
from the light of the stars.
I heard the scuttling
of gophers in their dark catacombs
& the distant hum of the aircraft factory
where my father was working the night shift.
The smell of the mouldering earth

& darkness enclosed me.
I peered out & saw my house
drifting away like a lily pad
on a dark pond. I cried out
but no one came. I slipped
into a sleepless dream—
my father was trying to reach me,
his legs churning like windmills
but he never got any closer—
my mother prayed while
her clasped hands burned
to a bouquet of bones.
I tasted ash & sang "Rock of Ages"
until there was no dream.

4.
This year there was no fire,
no poppies bloomed,
& I have never seen Hiroshima or Nagasaki.
Still I believe in the capitals
of the world
dark-suited men sit before
tumblers of ice water.
Their faces are stoic—
their gestures restrained—
but in their soft-cupped hands,
& in their closed fists,
they each hold a piece of that long night
into which our bones will burst
like white jasmine stars.

Pieces of Future

The question might have been
Why aren't there enough boats?
But it is too late for that question now,
we are five days out to sea, it is close to midnight,
& we are approaching an iceberg.
It is too late for my father to have second thoughts,
too late or too early in the century to lack faith in technology.

My mother cannot sleep. A cigarette burns
between her fingers as she tells me:
This is not a room. It's a confessional,
I can feel the weight of the water all around us—
an unsinkable ship flies in the face of God.
Later in life I would feel the same way about airplanes,
be conscious of air beneath my feet
whistling like the boy who cried wolf—
later in life I would know for certain
that there are people like my mother
with pieces of future already inside their brain.

My father says my mother is jinxing us, tells her:
Look at the craftsmanship, the glass dome
in the first class dining room—
the polished wood of the dance floor—
fix your mind on America.

Because of my mother's premonition,
her dream about the crow's nest,
the three bells sounding, I have begun
to consider the lifeboats, located them,
counted them. The wood of the lifeboats is
more real to me than the grey sheets
covering my bunk, the linen on the first class tables—
the deck chairs I am not allowed to sit in.

Women & children to the starboard side.
What of the men?
I have been thinking about this a lot.
Who should get into the boats first?

There will be no god by the boats
to look into our lives, who will be taken?
Who will know the stars by which to steer?
Who will row? Who divide the food,
the water, the warm coats?

My mother is bitter that we are in steerage.
She says she speaks better English
than anyone in first class, says I behave
at least as well as any child in second class.
There are things about us though
that make us more comfortable in the bottom of the boat.
My mother smokes, refuses to sleep.

Without my mother, my father
I will never get into a lifeboat.

Last night I dreamed about the ark.
There were two of everything
but the boat was taking water.
My father, who was also Noah,
was saying he would throw
one of each kind overboard.
Would he throw away the male or the female?
Some animals were crying.
I was a girl, I awaited my fate.

"The relief of rescue was tempered by a grim statistic: While all the children in first and second class were saved, two-thirds of the children in third class perished."
— "How We Found the Titanic," *National Geographic*, December 1985

3

Who shows a child as he really is? Who sets him
in his constellation and puts the measuring-rod
of distance in his hand? Who makes his death
out of gray bread, which hardens—or leaves it there
inside his round mouth, jagged as the core
of a sweet apple? . . . Murderers are easy to understand.
But this: that one can contain
death, the whole of death, even before
life has begun, can hold it to one's heart
gently, and not refuse to go on living,
is inexpressible.

         —Rainer Maria Rilke

Your
Being Beyond in the night
With words I fetched you back, there you are,
all is true and a waiting
for truth.

         —Paul Celan

The World

Wake to the sound of the woodpecker
vainly tapping the tarred roof,
& the greydead tree bejeweled
by a blowing mist. On the path
the incline causes the heart
to pump, the thigh to squeeze,
& everywhere the air is empty
of sound until bending to tie up
a loose lace you hear—
a million spotted ladybugs—
all the Whos in Whoville—
clinging, clambering,
humping like crazy—
rustling like dry leaves.
Turn back to the silence & the cabin
fetched by the smell of pinewood fire,
of green beans sautéing in anchovies & olive oil.
Know that the possibility
of pleasure is tenuous
& tangible as the slinky nightgown
hung on the nail, the Brut champagne
chilling in the refrigerator.

Viewed from this angle
the world is a picture window
through which many might choose
to enter. There is another window.
Sprayed with blood & marked by
a mother's hands sliding
all the way to the ground.
In the rot of that night
there are screams & cries
of the most loved ones—
then the crunch of the skull,
the slam of the screen door
then silence   till blood
wells up in a father's throat.
Then nothing—but the ache
of these arms that would carry away
all that is only ashes.
Both of these worlds exist.
There is no glass between them.

39

Paradox

Some say art brings order
to chaos, but what order
can this small poem bring
to the death of my parents—
to their brutal murders
in the dark of their own bedroom?
I notice how words still work
for my neighbors who barricade
themselves with their differences—
Oh it couldn't happen to me,
I have deadbolts on my door,
I don't drink, take my vitamins daily.
Some have even said
that *the lord has a plan.*

Well I say let my neighbors
turn under their wild garlic,
let them cut back the unruly
bramble or pokeweed,
in their place they can plant
rows of head lettuce
till kingdom come—theirs
is the wild card.
As for me, I will spread
lemon oil on the table,
slice vegetables into the soup,
invent an order for my children
in which they no longer believe.
When I asked the police lieutenant
for the thousandth time—
Why my parents?
he answered me exasperatedly
Why not your parents,
did you want someone else to die?
Neighbors, friends—life is a found penny.

Violence

In the dusty town of Anenecuilco,
birthplace of Emiliano Zapata,
the vote was spray-painted in red
on the wall of every intersection—
Cárdenas 757   Salinas 65.
The sky was a dark miasma—
the rain refused to fall.
Every seat on the bus was full,
but the aisles were clear
when the young girl got on & began to shout:
Mis padres estan muertos,
debo cuidar mis quatro hermanos,
no tengo ni dinero, ni trabajo,
esto es lo unico que se hacer—
My parents are dead,
I must take care of my 4 brothers & sisters,
I have no money, nor work,
this is the only think I know how to do.
Then she began to slowly insert
an icepick up her nose.
Though young boys swallow lighter fluid
& spit flames on too many corners here,
& a performance like this is not an uncommon sight—
her little brother collected coins
from even the poorest rider—
people called out to her to stop—
it was understood that this was an act
we would pay not to see.

*   *   *

Violence is in vogue.
It's cool to film
a serial killer, methodically
making no moral statement.
It's cool to let body parts float
to the surface of your text,
to frighten like the old joke,

like ivory soap. A writer I know
was delighted with a "found piece"—
a newspaper story which recounted
the odd words used by the victim
of a stabbing—*I felt the strange,*
cold object enter my body, it felt
like it belonged there.
Blood is colorful, is cowboy, is the last frontier.
Yippee yioo ki yay.

* * *

They came to the door wearing dark clothes. I mistook them for Jehova's
Witnesses. She was wearing a black pants suit, he a dark sports jacket. I
didn't see the badges at their waists. I answered their knock in an oversized
fuchsia sweatshirt my parents had given me on Christmas Eve. Seventeen
days earlier. I didn't want to let them in. They spoke obliquely, said it had
something to do with my sister. Once inside they told me my parents were
dead. Stabbed to death. My parents would lie in their chalk outlines for 15
hours. I never saw them again.

* * *

There is a "river of blood, wherein are boiling those
who live by violence and on others' fear."
What if, as in Dante's Inferno, there is consequence
for imagination as well as action?
Like the scientists doomed to see the dark
mushroom of their idea—what if writers too were consigned
to live among their own creations?
Ursula LeGuin says the only moral
we can put into fiction is hope.
Rough work inventing hope.

* * *

None of the booths were open at the fiesta in Tijuana. I persuaded myself I
could go with my friends to the cockfight to pass the time. Maybe I
thought I could watch a cockfight like Hemingway watched a bullfight.
Maybe I thought animals were a separate issue. I bought a Tecate & lit a
cigarette while two men in blood-sprayed T-shirts paraded the cocks around
the ring. The man on the loudspeaker kept yelling *Yeppa*. The man to the
left of me wore a cowboy hat, tooled boots & belt, drank Tecate too. He
stuffed a bill in the slit of a tennis ball, tossed it to the man taking bets. I

would have bet on the fat red cock, bet on peacock green, raven black,
flamingo red, the multicolored plumage of his tail. The man in the blood-
sprayed T-shirt only had to prop him up once, blow in his nostrils
once. Bet on beauty instead of death. The other cock, the fierce, wiry one,
pecked his eyes out in two minutes. *Yeppa.*

* * *

What can be said, after all, about pain?
That it comes in varying degrees?
So much of it can be prevented?
I have a friend who says
we should never have to feel pain
after the age of thirty-five.
Following this thought
she carries an array of medicines
in her bag—I once saw her
take codeine for a sunburn.
Cancer is a contract with pain.
Who among us, by now, has not
stood beside some hospital bed
& rubbed the scalp
or massaged the feet
of a loved one with the wild hope
that pleasure could balance pain?
This morning, while snatching
a dried bulb from a rose bush,
a thorn cut into my flesh—
deep & jagged.
I had to press my forefinger
to my thumb for an hour
to stop the bleeding.
The sudden pain took me by surprise,
would not go away, made me try
to quantify again
how much my parents had to feel.
To the end we are selfish children.
I have often wished out loud
that at least my mother
or at least my father might have lived.
But the truth is neither of them could have survived
the violence they saw done to each other.

* * *

I spread the seed on the ground
& go inside so the birds
feel free to descend.
First a jay, blue & aggressive,
helicopters in—
sunflower seeds or nothing
is his motto. Then the doves
flutter down, flutter down
so lightly they seem to slow time.
On the lip of the bird bath
a small sparrow lowers its beak—
perhaps she drinks with the water
her own clear image. These birds,
this impulse toward sustenance,
one clean, untroubled image,
mirror a world I wish we lived in.
Though driving to work yesterday,
fast, too fast, a dove glanced off
my windshield, crumpled to the street.
The balance of everything is so easily undone.

Tribute

Blind Bob's News Stand
kept long hours & my father
would walk there, sometimes
two times a day when he heard
a magazine was publishing my first poem.
It took weeks to arrive
& you would often see him
walking, wearing khaki shorts
that revealed the tangle
of varicose veins climbing his legs,
the blood rising, nevertheless,
in an orderly fashion,
entering now the left ventricle,
now the right. It comforts me
to think of his heart beating then,
you might say, just for me.
When my father was murdered
his blood pooled senselessly
beneath him, his big heart
pumping it farther & farther away
on a journey I can never follow
on a night I don't dare imagine.
How I wish when he finally
found that poem, he found at the top
some small dedication,
some tribute to how he labored for,
how he loved his six children.
& how I wish that out of the grey ash
that is his heart, he could rise to see
my love for him spilling senselessly,
pooling around the place his body should be.

Winter

Past winter solstice & one minute lighter every day.
I hate it. Hate this tilt toward summer,
hate the approach of spring,
the new green leaves with their glossy magazine finish.
Hate the bouncy way people start to walk—
the lists, the projects, the paint,
the ersatz youth in the air.

Never heliotropic,
I am in love with the pewtered sky,
bare antennae boughs
scratching at the scantiest ray of light.
On the third straight day of rain
I love the possibility of flood—
the mercurial drop—the frost warnings.

I love how everything resonates in me
as if winter were a house in which the past could live.
My mother could live. When I smoke cigarettes
I am my mother—when I feel pain I am my mother too.
I would like to be my mother when I hear a sad aria,
though she never heard one in her life, never will.
So then, I am just a daughter thinking of her mother—
did she love the winter, love the summer?

I make this poem so I can make a place
in which to love her.
The winter she embroidered
every one of my friends' names
in different colors on white blouse.
Gauche. I could never wear that blouse—
though I love the hands more than ever
that made each ropy stitch.

When my mother was murdered
there were 13 stab wounds to her left hand alone—
her index finger nearly sliced off—

Was it a kind of foreknowing
that gave her a highly developed sense of tragedy,

gave me my surest vocation?
Once, all eight of us were loaded into a station wagon
headed to Grandmother—California to Missouri.
As we left the driveway my mother said
"Turn back & look at your house, kids—
you may never see it again."

What no one seems to understand is
this winter soul, this craving for the dark, the cold,
the cellar being—is a kind of gift, a kind of nurturing—
what must happen is before us, until then
like a bulb in a paper sack
we must feed upon ourselves.
That is what my mother gave.
Yes, I will suffer, die—but, for now
I will live, unfurl even—at times, against my will—
like a goddamned yellow daffodil.

Prayer

if i have envied the bodies that bob & rock like rootless angels
float maskdown in the chillgreen if i have inclined toward dying
having imagined death to be like that i was a fool o mother o father
who no longer see what the divers see the dangle of brown seaweed
swaying like silk stockings the wash of pink coral jewelled garibaldi
across the green rock once in my neardrowning i desired i say sexual
i say insatiable more silence more rest was sucked by the deeper dimension
gulped water instead of air dreamed my death a 4 chambered nautilus
secreted yes like hair like nails all the used up days
(which are little deaths) transformed into iridescence yes but hard
shell too grief too pain weighing me down into pelagic depths
the beauty of the image calling me wrongly from the real   world
where once i swam in water so clear particles of dust settled on top
as if on a glass coffeetable & i have read that baudelaire's orgasms
were visual enough i say to deduce that the dead have no eyes no retina
(tho i have wished for them to see me) survive this trial by water
realize that death is no image rather the annihilation of all image
where once o once the bright world danced.

Dia de los Muertos

Some are taken with the notion of burning
the overrated scattering of ashes on sea—
my parents last appeared to me as names & dates
in delicate calligraphy on identical 8″ × 12″ boxes.
I have imagined, against my will,
the split second the mind can endure the image—
though there are worse things to imagine—
their beloved bodies burning. I prefer to rot.
Become part earth, part air, part grass blade,
part beetle-ingested molecule.
Give me the slow meltdown, a million metamorphoses.

* * *

There are places where the dead still have their day.
In the cemetery in San Miguel de Allende,
Lalo was speaking of November 2nd, *Dia de los Muertos*—
the one night the dead are given back on earth—
la banda plays *Las Golondrinas,*
friends & family clean the graves,
paint the tombstones lavender, white, shades of blue.
Xempatzuchitl, flowers of the dead,
are lain across the scrubbed tombs,
or are strewn on paths to help *los disfuntos* find their way home.
Behind the fake tiled wall,
behind the cold plaque of their names,
my parents are suddenly more dead than ever.
Lalo asked if we had any questions.
A woman from the states wearing SPF 30
& a sunhat she bought in New York with Mexico in mind asked:
"But do Mexicans feel sad when someone dies?"

* * *

October 28 is the day for those who
like my parents, died violently.
But the food & drink is placed outside the house
to keep these compromised spirits away.
After my parents were killed

49

the air was thick with their spirits—
they came to me in every dream
wrapped in blankets I feared to peel back—
rough creatures of Frankenstein with nails in their heads—
bloody signs of their unmaking.
Finally one night they appeared in baseball caps,
climbed into a yellow VW bus,
left me, they said, to travel the cosmos.
I kissed them goodbye.
Some people believe to go on grieving
chains the dead to this world.

*　*　*

But I love the idea, the possibility, of this carnal immortality—
sorrow yes, but joy, too, to have the loved ones
among us once again.
What special food shall I make for my parents?
They loved my salad—avocado, red onion,
tomato, romaine—still
I think they would rather drink.
I will toast their beige wall with vodka & orange juice.

To coax the dead close I think
you must study them passionately,
love them more than you were able
when they were alive.
What if my mother won't appear, won't come near,
unless my memory is perfect?
Was the mole on her neck to the left like mine,
or to the right of the gold fox necklace she wore?
Does she know I have finally balanced
the anger with the love?
My father—how little we ever really spoke,
& did we kiss goodbye
the last night before I drove away?
They will not return, even for one night—
all love is imperfect,
one of us cannot accept that.

*　*　*

What if you had just one night a year on earth?
What if you could taste food, smell flowers,

feel love? What if you were never sated in your lifetime?
Could you bear to touch with mortal hands
the ones who love you—then let them
fade into the fullness of their own lives?
Perhaps *la banda* would go on playing *Las Golondrinas*
& you would want to go on too
hearing voices weave your death & life in song.
Could you stand to taste, to swallow food
that could never fill you?
Wasn't this the way it was when you were alive?
Everything, everything always so near perfection,
so short of perfection. Perhaps my parents will return.

Where I Would Go

Even in the sparse forest
of the Cuyamacas, a part
of me is called out, called
beyond this trundling body
into a deeper green,
a chiller air. Then
like white wine hitting
an empty stomach,
the scent of the cedar incense,
the Jeffrey pines,
intoxicates me, melds
all five senses
into every surrounding
fleck & flash.
My feet sink deep,
already desirous
of their own destiny,
already surrendering
to the rich toss
of oak & pine.
The dank smell
of everything that decomposes
turns in me like the deepest change.
A day, a week, a month—
never enough—the parasite
in me wants nothing less
than to string itself
like dodderweed across the sinewy shrubs.
All that has died within me
would come out now
& graft itself onto this sure heaven—
hang forever
like green mistletoe
from the highest limb
of the leafless oak.

4

I say across the waves of the air to you:
today once more
I will try to be non-violent
one more day
this morning, waking the world away
in the violent day.

—Muriel Rukeyser

Halcyon

Driving home from work
a diamond-studded, football-shaped
spaceship appeared in the night sky—
hovered like a halo
above the southernmost part of the county.
I heard my own voice whisper
in the passengerless car—
Now this is something else.
Like a first star, like a wish,
I thought it was bringing my dead
back to me—perhaps, at the same moment
the man in the car next to me
believed, too, that the shining crescent
had entered the firmament
in direct relation to him—
he picked up the phone, began
talking & gesturing skyward—
the freeway turned to a field of brake lights,
we all stared up,
a kind of collective prayer
to its symmetry which suggested
the perfection we had all been seeking.
It was winter solstice
& we were desperate for fair weather,
desperate for convention to give way
to meaning, for the unfortunate earth
to be worthy of descent.
The man on the phone hung up
anyone might be lifted up at any time
the present was pure, absolute—
perhaps, lovers shivered in one another's arms again,
perhaps, his real estate properties plummeted.
Should we prepare ourselves for this god's eye—
drink clear water for three days,
or like escargot eat only corn meal for thirty days—
then begin the vertiginous descent
into ourselves, try to find the light
at the center?

Should we pack last things?
Bougainvillea blossoms, spaghetti & olive oil?
I was ready for astral intervention,
I was ready for the big change—
when the man on the radio said *Stop*—
Stop calling the police, the FBI, the Air Force base—
it's just a blimp trying out a new flight pattern—

soon it would wink/blink brand names down on us—
o yes, like the plaster of Paris gargoyle
I brought home from Carcassonne, like the Michelangelo
brought home from Rome, like Frito Lay—
it would be our souvenir, fiery opal, fiery opus—
halcyon in the sky—
our great glimmering, glamorous product
from the vast failure of the known.

Blue Silk Blouse

No sleep, no dreams,
no rain, no beauty.
The woman rises from her insomnia.
It is the dry season of the year,
the fourth year of the drought.
On what can she slake the thirst
of her body? On the cricket's
incidental song? On the color blue?
She thinks of the silk blouse
in the air-conditioned mall—
rises to that specific desire.
In the coyote-colored canyon
behind her house—
slated for development—
slated for a three-tiered mall—
she runs till her socks are filled with burrs,
till her eyes are sated with brown—
till her particular ghosts,
both dead & alive, lie still.

Blue haunts her thoughts again,
teal would be more accurate.
She remembers the insinuation
of grey among the threads.
Parched, abandoned snail shells
crunch beneath her feet
& the quantum culture of small things—
ticks, fleas, mice, lizards—
rearrange themselves around her step.
Thirst is audible in this barren sea,
in this ocean of ugly.
Jackrabbits scatter into the sparse shadow of greasewood,
sweat rings her armpits, diamonds her back.
The field is a spent economy—
tractors & backhoes are the horizon.
She things again of silk
sliding across her skin, the blouse
is a cool pool, an oasis
in this dry patch of disturbed land.

Suddenly a chance bloom rises
almost purple, almost violet
from the center of the burnt-out buckwheat.
That night she dreams her own face
in the mirror in the mall—
out of skin tanned canyon brown
a mouth breaks, blossoms bougainvillea—
dragonflies & feathers fly from her lips—
the canyon ciphers her being—
her body the source of infinite surprise.

Next day in the mall
she is Anna Karenina, reckless
before the train, insatiable
before the array. Each purchase
equals something, someone lost.
In her hand she carries a bag
with a blue silk blouse,
in her head a list of all she wishes to buy—
& if tomorrow six-foot tires tear
the Gypsy tents, the midnight webs
of red canyon spiders—
what can save her from
the catalogue of her future?

"Things are in the Saddle and Ride Mankind"
—Emerson

I was riding myself like a horse,
I was lathered in the sun,
she was screaming on the downtown sidestreet,
I was walking, my car was broken,
my blue shoes were marching
matching a maroon & blue–striped dress.
I thought I looked self-contained
but I knew what she knew—
to walk is to parade is to be exposed
I was exposed, her voice was undoing me.

I am a cracked egg
my essence could seep
from any orifice,
could escape in a tear,
a dribble of urine,
a scream.

*See the funny astronauts
burning up in space . . .*

Blue shoes on the sidewalk hurt
me walking too fast too straight
riding high for a fall . . .

*See the funny astronauts
burning up in space . . .*

The madsanity of her vision
might pierce anyone, the debris
of technology falling all around.
My car was irreparable. She had
cut the toes out of her shoes.

What can I tell you to make you care
about me? That we are alike. That
on that day in the sun I was alone I
was worldweary I was breaking down
that sleep & alcohol had failed me.
Maybe those are the wrong things

but would it matter? I sometimes
think I could never be touched
enough. That is my plea. Yet
the woman walking so close to me
was screaming & I cared & I did
no thing.

I saw how we were alike
the future having fallen away
from us so suddenly we had lost
the godedenmarxutopia
of tomorrow & the sun was .
shining mercilessly boiling
the spit on the sidewalk

eatsleepworkshopeatsleepworkshop
eatsleepworkshopmakeloveeatsleep
workshopmakeloveeatsleepworkshop
die

Desire in disorder
life becomes a list:
1. pay insurance
2. pick up cat food
3. phone lover
4. grade papers
5. send thank you cards
6. call neptune society

My own desire for a better world
has become lost, converted, perverted . . .
like that of the suburban peacock
perched on the shakeshingle roof
who pierced the semisilence
with his unrequited call
descending into the real world
to dance before a fire hydrant,
before a dog, before me—
shivering his gleaming feathers—
I was not unmoved.

But imagine a sunny day ozone
intact, production organized for
humanneed. There are more trees

in this picture—leafy chestnuts, shady oaks—fewer cars. Two women pass on the street. Maybe they smile. One is on her way to the Center City Arts Building where she has a studio, everyone being urged to take one for at least a quarter of the year. She has just finished her obligatory 4 hours at the Center for Accordant Technology. In her pocket she fingers a list: change daycare pickup, meet Addis Community Kitchen 7:00. The other woman has just experienced a tragedy of some dimension & as is the custom in certain Native American tribes she will be cared for by the community for one year. More if necessary.

On a sidewalk a greyhaired woman
& a brownhaired woman are walking.
They are adjacent to one another.
They are not in relation to one another.

weltshmerz = mental depression or apathy caused by comparison of the actual state of the world with an ideal state

Or imagine that two women are passing on a dirty treeless street. One is screaming the other is frightened she will scream. The sun is shining & they are both subject to premature skin cancer. The one woman lives in the undulating aftershock of violent death. The other was just released from County Mental Health because, after all, she is incurable.

Or this—
the woman & the woman spoke,
touched, but could not help nor
heal one another. The woman
& the peacock copulated.
Children were born with
stunning green godseyes in
their foreheads or tails.
In certain cities, until it all
came to an end, streetscreaming
& roofcawing became an accepted
mode of communication.

I Write My Future

1. Mean-Spirited Present

A man, a woman, & two children
are crossing a long stretch of sand.
The ocean shimmers
cool in the distance.
(This is not a metaphor.)
Offshore & unseen
a nuclear submarine passes.
The family is feeling
five days in paradise
& why aren't we happy?
Their progress is slowed
because the woman insists
on stopping to pick up
bits of Styrofoam & plastic,
pieces of glass that glint
green or brown in the pale sand.
She feels she is righting
some larger wrong.
(Which one o cup to the Titanic?)
The man pauses patiently,
but feels no inclination
to pick up after others.
She thinks perhaps he
is waiting for the one absolute
correct thing to do.
They have come so far together
& the children are hopping
from shadow to shadow—
the hot sand blistering
the soles of their little feet.

2. The Uncertainty Principle

My fingers hesitate over the keys.
What if this computer
tapped into my lifeline,
& I, unwittingly, cast my own die?
Or there is this—
like a small quantum of light
focused on a moving particle
this poem could alter the course
of the life it chooses to examine—
split my marriage down its weak seam,
cause my children to turn from me,
or my work to abandon me?

3. This is not a story.

It is the middle of a life
recounted in a poem—
there is some anxiety,
as if before a live sporting event,
for the outcome is unknown.
Begin anywhere—
the past is continuous,
the present displaced—
in the future images tremble
& rearrange themselves like molecules
waiting for us to become them.

4. Lush Past

Two years ago
I rose up out of my sleep.
I was light, aerated,
particles with the darkness.
Expectation filled me like helium—
the thought came to me
from outside myself—
happiness is coming toward you.
There was no hint, then, of the tragedy
just around the corner.

5. October 12, 1999

Woke to the sound of fogdrops off the eaves. Was clearheaded, energetic, as
if I got the chemicals right, just enough to drink last night. When I went
out to fill the birdfeeder thought for the thousandth time of Sally. Her
remonstrance: If you begin to feed wild birds you must commit yourself,
they become dependent on you. Thought for the thousandth time how
Sally loves to make the world depend on her—how much we are alike. The
grass beneath my feet was moist & cold. My fiftieth birthday. My wish is
to have white wine & salmon studded with peppercorns, my family at my
table. Smile to myself to imagine the next century, having predicted doom
since 1979. How observable at last, for me, the forces are. Evil is large,
looms. Hope/kindness small, hard to see, everywhere. & the simple hue of
trees, sky, water—a kind of glue that holds it all together. I send this
message of hope to my children to sustain them in their darkest hour.

6. A Small Piece of Sage

What if happiness travelled
like light from the stars?
What if that happiness
emitted toward me so long ago
finally reached me?
Small particles of spontaneous luminosity
settle into my very being,
I begin to give off light,
am clothed in color.
What if not only the world
is beautiful (so beautiful
that the scent of a small piece of sage
can save you), but what if, at last,
my life achieved a kind of beauty?

Utopia

Grey, grey, the color of extinction
or winter limbs or mourning doves was in my head.
Hungover, smoked out, all undeserving
of a minor miracle, a suburban revelation.
Still a pyramid-shaped hive, abuzz with a thousand bees,
rose before me in the field.
The swirling architecture, circled,
curled like ribboned candy,
turned in upon itself—refused linearity.
Honey was the smell.
I crouched two feet away
listened to the sounds of community,
saw the tiny holes, pale yellow wax—
beebodies crawling in & out,
swarming over one another,
wings beating heat for everyone.
I looked for the queen,
a long train, a diadem, perhaps
she was sealed in the inner sanctum,
Aida entombed with her doomed lover,
or just above me, mating on the wing,
then the drone swooning groundward,
the inevitable gravity. Deathward.
In the center of the field a beekeeper
kept fifty "official" hives, they hummed
in complicity with him—but here
fleshed into a tobacco tree & tumbleweed
renegade bees & a breakaway queen
had built their own golden Gaudi cathedral.

What I need now is earth—or Alice
to offer me a mushroom, a square of windowpane,
a toke from the hookah, to shrink me
the size of a bee—let me be
wild as buckwheat, as clover—
taste, just once, collective,
the orgasm, the honeyflow.